Rescue

Praying for Your Teen in a Drowning Culture

Prayer Journal

CANDY GIBBS

Scripture quotations, unless otherwise noted
are taken from THE HOLY BIBLE, NEW INTER-
NATIONAL VERSION, NIV®Copyright© 1973,
1978, 1984, 2011 by Bilica, Inc.® Used by per-
mission. All rights reserved worldwide.

Fedd Books
401 Ranch Rd. 620 S
Ste. 250
Austin, TX 78734
www.thefeddagency.com

ISBN: 978-0-9907044-7-8

Printed in the United States of America
First Edition 10 9 8 7 6 5 4 3 2 1

INTRODUCTION

"For though we live in the world, we do not wage war as the world does. The weapons we fight with are not the weapons of the world. On the contrary, they have divine power to demolish strongholds. We demolish arguments and every pretension that sets itself up against the knowledge of God, and we take captive every thought to make it obedient to Christ." 2 Corinthians 10:3-6

My Bible literally falls open to the page containing this life preserver that I have clung to more sleepless nights than I can count. *The weapons we fight with...have divine power to demolish strongholds.* As the parents of teens, we can become desperate for weapons effective in tearing down the strongholds the culture would

i

inflict upon our children: attacks against their faith and their relationship with their own family, perverted sexuality, and access to pornography through the Internet. With wave after wave crashing down on us, we must have a weapon, a life preserver, to take hold of to help us weather the onslaught of the enemy.

"We demolish arguments and every pretension that sets itself up against the knowledge of God." Aren't we thankful that we have been given a weapon to demolish arguments and pretensions that set themselves up against our God? On almost a daily basis, we see posts on social media, comments made by celebrities, or advertisements that mock God and all that He represents. Our teens are encouraged to set their heroes in a higher place than God. They are taught to put their own desires above His. Our culture indoctrinates them to consider themselves before anyone else. They are told they are the center of the universe

and should do whatever makes them happy. And, oh my, fear can surely set in for parents. *What if our children make the wrong choice? Do the wrong thing? Hang with the wrong people? What if no likes them? Or what if everyone does?* All these thoughts are arguments and pretensions that set themselves up against the Lord's very words, *"For I know the plans I have for you declares the Lord, plans to prosper you and not to harm you, plans to give you hope and a future."* Jeremiah 29:11

I can vividly remember a certain morning I spent with the Father, and there was nothing pretty about it. For hours I was on my face, sobbing and bargaining with Him. I begged Him to change things with one of my children. I repented of every sin and shortcoming I could recall. I promised to do anything He asked of me. I whispered and shouted. I cried and prayed.

And when I had soaked tears clear

through my rug and my entire being was completely exhausted—I listened. He whispered, in His all too familiar fashion, to my heart, "This is not about you having control. You are not in control of your children, and any thought to the contrary is a mirage. I am also not interested in your begging and empty promises. This is about *my promises* and your willingness to have enough faith to believe them."

It was then that I began to realize that my only course of action that would have any impact on my children lay in *how* I related to my Father. Now when I pray and when I trust Him, He calms the storms and makes the winds and the waves still for my babies.

I would not say that morning was pretty—but it was most certainly beautiful.

I am honored and humbled to embark on this journey with you. I will stand with you in the gap for our children through prayer. The Lord will fight for us; we need only be still and trust in Him.

Candy

1

Becoming a
Rescue Swimmer

"As Pharaoh approached, the Israelites looked up, and there were the Egyptians marching after them. They were terrified....Moses answered the people, "Do not be afraid. Stand firm and you will see the deliverance the Lord will bring you today. The Egyptians you see today you will never see again. The Lord will fight for you; you need only to be still.... Then the Lord said to Moses...."

Exodus 14:10, 13-15

I've always wondered what Moses was thinking at that point. Right between "you need only to be still" and "Then the Lord said." Moses had just led the Israelites out of captivity; the sand from

1

all the Egyptian brick making was still in their eyes and under their fingernails. Moses must have still been trying to gather his thoughts enough to determine what they might eat and how on earth he would manage the starts and stops with this multitude. When he found himself with his toes up to the water's edge of the Red Sea and Pharaoh and his army on his heels, how did he feel in *that* moment?

I wonder, because as parents of teens, we will often find ourselves caught between an approaching enemy and a raging sea. While I may not truly be able to relate to how Moses felt, I have a keen understanding of the sensation that "there is no good and perfect way out of *this* one and someone may get hurt." What I am asking the Father, for you and me both, is that rather than being overcome by dread when our toes feel that cool sensation of the sea, we would realize that those moments—the ones that are hopeless and overwhelming—are the perfect backdrop for the miraculous.

Lord Jesus, thank You that You are in the business of calming the wind and the waves. We come against fear and apprehension in Your mighty name and we thank You that we can face these crazy seas of the teen years as long as we follow You! Make us strong and wise. We love You.

PRAYER JOURNAL

Comfort, comfort my people says your God....Every valley shall be raised up, every mountain and hill made low; the rough ground shall become level, the rugged places a plain.

Isaiah 40:1;3-4

_____

_____

_____

_____

_____

_____

_____

_____

There is no doubt we live in a culture that is counter to biblical principle and counter to the values that are important to you as you raise your families.

He tends his flock like a shepherd: He gathers the lambs in his arms and carries them close to his heart; he gently leads those that have young.

Isaiah 40:11

_____

_____

_____

_____

_____

_____

_____

_____

_____

_____

Our rescue, our redemption, our hope will be found in Him alone.

Candy Gibbs

But those who hope in the Lord will renew their strength.

Isaiah 40:31

_____

_____

_____

_____

_____

_____

_____

_____

_____

_____

_____

Let's step up on top of the waves of perversion, immorality, fear, and insecurity. Let's focus on Him and follow Him.

6

On the earth, nations will be in anguish and perplexity at the roaring and tossing of the sea. People will faint from terror, apprehensive of what is coming on the world, for the heavenly bodies will be shaken. At that time they will see the Son of Man coming in a cloud with power and great glory.

Luke 21:25-27

_____

_____

_____

_____

_____

_____

_____

_____

_____

Take courage. Get out of the boat and believe in Him.

But Jesus immediately said to them: "Take courage! It is I. Don't be afraid." "Lord, if it's you," Peter replied, "tell me to come to you on the water." "Come," he said. Then Peter got down out of the boat, walked on the water and came toward Jesus.

Matthew 14:27-29

_____

_____

_____

_____

_____

_____

_____

_____

_____

Let's learn the warning signs for our teens so that we are not caught off guard by the drowning culture.

A furious squall came up, and the waves broke over the boat, so that it was nearly swamped. Jesus was in the stern, sleeping on a cushion. The disciples woke him and said to him, "Teacher, don't you care if we drown?" He got up, rebuked the wind and said to the waves, "Quiet! Be still!" Then the wind died down and it was completely calm.

Mark 4:37-40

_____

_____

_____

_____

_____

_____

Perfection is not the goal. The goal is to learn to turn our gaze toward Him even in the midst of violent seas and overwhelming waves.

Candy Gibbs

He said to his disciples, 'Why are you so afraid? Do you still have no faith?' They were terrified and asked each other, 'Who is this? Even the wind and the waves obey him!'

Mark 4: 41

_____

_____

_____

_____

_____

_____

_____

_____

_____

_____

Parenting is not about how our children respond to us; it is much more about how we respond to the Lord.

2

Praying for Your Family

"For this reason I remind you to fan into flame the gift of God, which is in you through the laying on of my hands. For the Spirit God gave us does not make us timid, but gives us power, love and self-discipline."

2 Timothy 1:6-7

We must not not afraid. It is as simple as that. We do not have time to be fearful about the day in which we are living, what will happen tomorrow, or if our teens will rebel if we set boundaries. I am convinced that fear is one of the most powerful weapons of the enemy—possibly his most powerful. He has made us scared to take a stand, too faint-hearted to trust God for the outcome, and afraid to hope that tomorrow will be better. But no more.

There is nothing closer to the heart of parents than their family. Praying for your family can seem like a last resort, a defensive response to an attack of the enemy. Many prayers I have offered for my family over the years have been in times of desperation and fear over the current situation or a dreamed-up horrific scenario about what lay around the corner. Prayer for my family has often been done in private, in whispers, with tears streaming down my face.

But let me assure you, when you take a knee at 5:00 a.m. with a cup of coffee, your robe, and your Bible, the scene may seem very "Norman Rockwell" to you. But the enemy's view is something quite different: you look like David, full of unabashed belief in the Most High, walking onto a battlefield in God's armor—His Word as your sword and your words of praise and adoration to your God a war cry in the enemy's ears. You are unafraid and standing your ground on behalf of those you love.

Lord, I ask You to protect our families. I thank You, Father, that You have given Your angels charge of them. You go before and behind them. You have armed us for battle and we are not afraid. You have given us Your Spirit of power, love, and a sound mind. I thank You that our families are called to make an impact, and we take an offensive posture against our enemy. Lord, grant our families favor, influence, boldness, and strength to declare Your Great Name and goodness to all. Thank You, Father that You appoint Your love and faithfulness to protect our families. We trust You to protect, guide, and direct them and use them as You will for Your glory. We love you.

PRAYER JOURNAL

When your children grasp for something to
hold on to in the middle of a storm, they
will reach for the anchor of your family.

_____

_____

_____

_____

_____

_____

_____

_____

_____

*Put on the full armor of God, so that you
can take your stand against the devil's
schemes.*

Ephesians 6:11

Rescue Prayer Journal

Teens often have some level of insecurity;
be an encourager, be a safe place.

_____

_____

_____

_____

_____

_____

_____

_____

_____

_____

_____

_____

*Children are a heritage from the Lord,
offspring a reward from him.*
Psalm 127:3

Candy Gibbs

Our homes should be places of peace and refuge. Learn to fight for peace in your home.

_____

_____

_____

_____

_____

_____

_____

_____

_____

_____

_____

Choose for yourselves this day whom you will serve....But as for me and my household, we will serve the Lord.

Joshua 24:15b

Rescue Prayer Journal

Peace is worth fighting for. Peace is critical. Our children need it and we need it.

_____

_____

_____

_____

_____

_____

_____

_____

_____

_____

Listen, my son, to your father's instruction and do not forsake your mother's teaching.

Proverbs 1:8

Candy Gibbs

Set standards for your children to protect
their dignity, character and then hold
your ground.

_____

_____

_____

_____

_____

_____

_____

_____

_____

_____

*I pray not that you should take them out
of the world, but that you should keep
them from the evil one.*

John 17:1

Families are as unique as snowflakes, all with their own charm, and you won't find another exactly like yours. Still, not one of them is perfect.

_____

_____

_____

_____

_____

_____

_____

_____

_____

_____

A perfect family isn't the goal—the goal is loving well and being authentic.

Candy Gibbs

Do not conform to the pattern of this world, but be transformed by the renewing of your mind. Then you will be able to test and approve what God's will is—his good, pleasing and perfect will.

Romans 12:2

_____

_____

_____

_____

_____

_____

_____

_____

_____

Love the Lord. Love your family. Seek first His kingdom and He will take care of all things.

3

Praying for Your Teen's Faith and Identity

What moves you? Recently, I participated in a Bible study, Children of the Day, by Beth Moore on 1 and 2 Thessalonians. One of the topics we discussed was all the hardships the apostle Paul faced. He was stripped, beaten, stoned, severely flogged, imprisoned, and shipwrecked, and he faced death on more than one occasion. And yet, he continued. That is what you call determination. I hate to admit it, but it would have taken just the first stripping to convince me that I had missed God. He must have meant for me to spend the week on a beach instead. All kidding aside, don't we yearn for a calling and purpose so clear in our heart and mind that we would be determined to see it through?

So do our teens. They desire to know who they are and whose they are. They may not always know the right way to go about that discovery, but they want to believe in something greater than themselves and to serve a great purpose. Your prayers as parents are so important. Faith is such a funny thing. The way we develop faith in the Father is by being in a needy, sometimes frightening situation, and then seeing Him walking on the waves in precisely our direction. Personally, the seasons of my life when I have been shipwrecked, water-logged, freezing, and seemingly alone have produced the deepest rooted, strongest areas of faith in the depths of my being. Though I often didn't enjoy the experiences, I wouldn't trade the lessons I learned about His character for anything. It was in those moments that my faith became my own.

As parents, we must realize that our children need those same moments. Moments when waves come and it's cold, lonely, and sometimes dark. Only when they have been cold can they appreciate a warm blanket. Only when they have been hungry can they appreciate a home cooked meal. And only when they have experienced the uncertainty of a raging sea, can they appreciate a Savior who walks on water—and then faith becomes their own.

Lord, may we so desire to see our children serve You, our spouses winning people for the Kingdom, and the hungry fed and the lost found with such passion that we trust You in the process. May none of these things move us from our course—determined to see Your kingdom come on earth as it is in heaven. Lord, make us a pure and spotless bride, ready for her bridegroom—full of spunk, righteousness, boldness, strength, gentleness, and peace. We love you.

PRAYER JOURNAL

...Therefore have I set my face like flint, and I know I will not be put to shame.

Isaiah 50:7b

_____

_____

_____

_____

_____

_____

_____

_____

_____

Encourage your teen to read Scripture. The Word will build them up and remind them of who they are.

So God created mankind in his own image, in the image of God he created them; male and female he created them.

Genesis 1:27

_____

_____

_____

_____

_____

_____

_____

_____

_____

_____

Encouraging teens to attend church on Sundays and go to summer camp with their youth group is not the same as praying for them to have a personal relationship with Christ.

Candy Gibbs

*Therefore, if anyone is in Christ, the new
creation has come: The old has gone; the
new is here!*
2 Corinthians 5:17

_____

_____

_____

_____

_____

_____

_____

_____

_____

_____

Modeling a personal relationship with
Christ can encourage your teen to swim
out alone into the deeper waters of faith
in Him.

But you are a chosen people, a royal priesthood, a holy nation, God's special possession, that you may declare the praises of him who called you out of darkness into his wonderful light.

I Peter 2:9

_____

_____

_____

_____

_____

_____

_____

_____

Teaching your teen to find value and identity in the Lord is more critical than teaching them to eat healthy and helping them get into the university of their choice.

Candy Gibbs

You were taught, with regard to your former way of life, to put off your old self, which is being corrupted by its deceitful desires; to be made new in the attitude of your minds; and to put on the new self, created to be like God in true righteousness and holiness.

Ephesians 4:22-24

_____

_____

_____

_____

_____

_____

_____

_____

_____

Pray scripture over your teen at night.

I have been crucified with Christ and I no longer live, but Christ lives in me. The life I now live in the body, I live by faith in the Son of God, who loved me and gave himself for me.

Galatians 2:20

_____

_____

_____

_____

_____

_____

_____

_____

_____

Set the bar high. Great
expectations give our teens
something for which to strive for.

Candy Gibbs

As the rain and snow come down from heaven, and do not return to it without watering the earth and making it bud and flourish, so that it yields seeds for the sower and bread for the eater, so is my word that goes out from my mouth: It will not return to me empty, but will accomplish what I desire and achieve the purpose for which I sent it.

Isaiah 55:11

_____

_____

_____

_____

_____

_____

_____

Your teen is a beloved child of the King who may be gifted in many different things. Remind them of their calling. Validate the things they have seen God do in their own lives.

4

Praying for Your Teen's Purity and Future Spouse

Now Isaac had come from Beer Lahai Roi, for he was living in the Negev. He went out to the field one evening to meditate, and as he looked up, he saw camels approaching. Rebekah also looked up and saw Isaac. She got down from her camel and asked the servant, "Who is that man in the field coming to meet us?" "He is my master," the servant answered. So she took her veil and covered herself. The servant told Isaac all he had done. Isaac brought her into the tent of his mother Sarah, and he married Rebekah. So she became his wife and he loved her.

Genesis 24:62-67a

31

So she took her veil and covered her-self. I love that. Purity.

Sometimes in a culture that screams "Do what thou wilt" without any regret or consequence, the thought of a purity so authentic as for a young woman to veil her face when she sees her future husband for the first time almost escapes us. But how romantic—to actually leave something to be desired, something untouched. When Isaac married Rebekah, none of his household (except the servant who found her), had ever seen her beauty—none before Isaac.

I also love that Rebekah caught a glimpse of Isaac when he was still afar off. In the years of waiting, when your teen son is anxious to know what she will look like, or your daughter what he enjoys doing—in the years of waiting, when we as parents beg the Lord to take great care in choosing just the one for our girl or when we ask Him to please keep her hidden well enough that no one would misuse or mistreat her before she meets our boy—in those waiting years, I pray that He would allow us a glimpse from afar to encourage and remind us that He is a true romantic. He is the author of history's most beautiful love stories, and He has most certainly not forgotten our children.

Lord, help us to teach our teens the beauty and the power of purity. Help us to believe You for our children's coming spouses and trust that You have their very best interests at heart. We know You will never let us down. You desire to give them the desire of their hearts, and it is beautiful. There is power that comes with purity as well. A person who allows You to veil their heart in waiting and who trusts You to develop in them self-control and character, will see the power of Your presence in their marriage. And Lord, as you continue to script the love story for my teens, I know

You are aware of how very much this mom loves them. It's hard for a mama who has wiped tears and doctored bruised knees and bruised egos to release those holy duties to another. But I will do it, Lord, because I know that You have prepared a young man to be my daughter's prince and You have fashioned a young lady to veil her heart for my son. I trust You with their purity and with their promises. We pray for that kind of love for our teens. Someday, Lord. We love You.

PRAYER JOURNAL

Let the king be enthralled by your beauty;
honor him, for he is your lord.
Psalm 45:11

_____

_____

_____

_____

_____

_____

_____

_____

_____

Thank God today because He is the author and creator of love and intimacy.

Do not conform to the pattern of this world, but be transformed by the renewing of your mind. Then you will be able to test and approve what God's will is—his good, pleasing and perfect will.

Romans 12:2

_____

_____

_____

_____

_____

_____

_____

_____

_____

_____

God is love. He understands it; He relates to us through it; He embodies it.

But you are a chosen people, a royal priesthood, a holy nation, God's special possession, that you may declare the praises of him who called you out of darkness into his wonderful light.

I Peter 2:9

_____

_____

_____

_____

_____

_____

_____

_____

_____

_____

The enemy loves to steal from our children the innocence and beauty of sex shared only between a husband and a wife.

But in your hearts revere Christ as Lord. Always be prepared to give an answer to everyone who asks you to give the reason for the hope that you have. But do this with gentleness and respect, keeping a clear conscience, so that those who speak maliciously against your good behavior in Christ may be ashamed of their slander. For it is better, if it is God's will, to suffer for doing good than for doing evil.

I Peter 3: 15-17

_____

_____

_____

_____

_____

_____

_____

We must discuss hard issues with our children, be open about our own struggles, and encourage them to struggle well.

Flee from sexual immorality. All other sins a person commits are outside the body, but whoever sins sexually, sins against their own body.

I Corinthians 6:18

_____

_____

_____

_____

_____

_____

_____

_____

_____

_____

Be confident in your own calling as a parent. You are the gatekeeper of your home.

No temptation has overtaken you except what is common to mankind. And God is faithful; he will not let you be tempted beyond what you can bear. But when you are tempted, he will also provide a way out so that you can endure it.

I Corinthians 10:13

_____

_____

_____

_____

_____

_____

_____

_____

_____

Don't be afraid to set boundaries for your teen and communicate why they are important.

It is God's will that you should be sanctified: that you should avoid sexual immorality; that each of you should learn to control your own body in a way that is holy and honorable, not in passionate lust like the pagans, who do not know God....
                    Thessalonians 4:3-5

_____

_____

_____

_____

_____

_____

_____

_____

_____

Pray for your teen's friends, friends of friends, parents of friends—all to remain pure.

5

Praying for Your Teen's Purity in Using Technology

"For though we live in the world, we do not wage war as the world does. The weapons we fight with are not the weapons of the world. On the contrary, they have divine power to demolish strongholds. We demolish arguments and every pretension that sets itself up against the knowledge of God, and we take captive every thought to make it obedient to Christ."

2 Corinthians 10:3-5

"The Spirit of the Lord God is upon me; because the Lord hath anointed me to preach good tidings unto the

meek; he hath sent me to bind up the brokenhearted, to proclaim liberty to the captives, and the opening of the prison to them that are bound...."

Isaiah 61:11 (KJV)

To proclaim liberty to the captives. What an interesting thought as we cover our children in prayer regarding their use of technology. Captives can be bound by many things. It does not take a 50 pound chain to entangle a 13-year-old child It is easily done with an iPhone, iTouch, iPad. Maybe the problem is the iGeneration? Could it be that we have unknowingly allowed them to become bound up and taken captive within themselves?

We have all seen movies depicting someone in a cold, dark prison cell huddled in a corner—trapped and alone. Conjure up that image in your mind. Now see with your mind's eye, your teenager around 8:00p.m. See them crouched on the corner of the couch, phone in hands, having no interaction with your family, not even looking up except to watch television or play another video game. Not a lot of difference in those two scenarios—one bound by the enemy's chains and behind his bars, and the other bound by the chain of the enemy we bought them for Christmas last year.

Technology can be greatly beneficial, but for many of our teenagers and children it has become a prison. We would not stand by as our children were literally carried into captivity, but often we not only stand by and allow it spiritually, but we enable and encourage it. Because truth be told, sometimes we serve the same master.

Technology should provide a way for our families to gain information, to stay connected with those who do not live near us, to communicate quickly when necessary. It should not be a prison cell that is deadening our social skills, creating a generation that can't give a firm handshake or look others in the eye, or even feel comfortable making a simple phone call. We are losing an understanding of true friendship and relationship. Our years with our teens are short and priceless. The Lord has come to set us free from all of our captors. Take Him up on it now.

Lord, we do come against every argument and pretension that would set itself up against the knowledge of Your son, our Christ. Help us, Father, to swim victoriously in the dark, deep, and cold waters of technology. We ask, Lord, that our family would not be bond-servants to anything or anyone but You. We love You first, we love You most and will allow nothing to set itself in a higher position than You. You are truly the Most High. God, make us bold. Make us wise. We choose You. I love You.

PRAYER JOURNAL

Finally, brothers and sisters, whatever is true, whatever is noble, whatever is right, whatever is pure, whatever is lovely, whatever is admirable—if anything is excellent or praiseworthy—think about such things.

Philippians 4:8

_____

_____

_____

_____

_____

_____

_____

Ask the Lord to give you directions with boundaries, and commit to abide by the set boundaries.

But I tell you that anyone who looks at a woman lustfully has already committed adultery with her in his heart.

Matthew 5:28

_____

_____

_____

_____

_____

_____

_____

_____

_____

_____

Be aware of putting your teen in adult situations far too early, before he or she is equipped to handle them.

Do not conform to the pattern of this world, but be transformed by the renewing of your mind. Then you will be able to test and approve what God's will is—his good, pleasing and perfect will.

Romans 12:2

_____

_____

_____

_____

_____

_____

_____

_____

_____

I want to encourage you—you are the parent of your child. Don't fall to pressure from this culture. You decide what is allowed in your own home.

*For I have chosen him, so that he will
direct his children and his household
after him to keep the way of the LORD by
doing what is right and just.*

Genesis 18:19a

_____

_____

_____

_____

_____

_____

_____

_____

_____

Savor every moment you have with your
family. Don't allow them unfettered
access to technology.

Candy Gibbs

All the ways of the LORD are loving and faithful toward those who keep the demands of his covenant.

Psalm 25: 10

_____

_____

_____

_____

_____

_____

_____

_____

_____

_____

_____

When it comes to technology, balance and boundaries are imperative.

Rescue Prayer Journal

As parents, we too need not be con-
sumed with social media.   We must set
the example.

_____

_____

_____

_____

_____

_____

_____

_____

_____

_____

_____

_____

*Be joyful in hope, patient in affliction,
faithful in prayer.*

Romans 12:12

Candy Gibbs

Put your phone down, step away from the computer, and spend quality time with your family. There is absolutely no substitute for time.

_____

_____

_____

_____

_____

_____

_____

_____

_____

_____

_____

Your teen is wired up, synced up, connected to, and interacting with a very large community. Shouldn't he or she be tuned into the Father? Synced up with your family and values?

6

Praying for Your Teen's Biblical Stance on Homosexuality

"But he said to me, 'My grace is sufficient for you, for my power is made perfect in weakness.' Therefore I will boast all the more gladly about my weaknesses, so that Christ's power may rest on me. That is why for Christ's sake, I delight in weaknesses, in insults, in hardships, in persecutions, in difficulties. For when I am weak, then I am strong."

2 Corinthians 12:9-10

Remember those teachers you had who went above and beyond, who loved their job so much and took their responsibility to train the next generation so seriously that they would make several different versions of the same test so everyone sitting near each other would have a test unique to them? I can recall talking with friends over lunch who had already been to that particular class that morning and asking about the test. By the time the lunch period was over, I had assessed my options and I knew with certainty which version of the test I did not want.

And there were those times when I would sit down in my chair, pen in hand, and a cold sweat would come over me as I realized that the test with my name at the top was precisely the one I had so hoped to avoid.

In working on the book Rescue and now the devotional, I can tell you what has been most important to me is that I be honest and authentic. As I live and breathe, the first test that I hope I'm never asked to take is to lose one of my children to either an addiction or death.

The second is this one right here. In being completely honest, I am weak, and ask the Lord not to write my name on this evaluation. I bet you feel the same way. As a matter of fact, if your sweet name is at the top of a test dealing with a child struggling with homosexuality, I believe you feel the same way too. No one wants this one. And no one wants this one for anyone else either.

If you have never dealt with a child of yours struggling with homosexuality, it's important to remember that we must offer grace and support to those parents who are in such a situation. What if you asked those parents if you could walk with them and pray together for all your children? Don't suddenly avoid them or treat them differently. We must pray for them and come alongside them as they take the test of their lifetime.

If you are a parent dealing with a teen struggling with homosexuality, I want to remind you that your love for your child is not dependent on lifestyle or obedience. Your love, like the Father's, is unconditional. Your hope is in Him. You must keep your eyes glued on Him. You simply take the next step with Him. He will never leave you or forsake you. Do not give in to hopelessness.

"Love is patient, love is kind. It does not envy, does not boast, it is not proud. It is not rude, it is not self-seeking, it is not easily angered, it keeps no record of wrongs. Love does not delight in evil but rejoices with the truth. Love protects, always trusts, always hopes, always perseveres. Love never fails."
1 Corinthians 13:4-8a

I was recently on a panel with a pastor who was asked the question, "What would you do if you had a 14-year-old son who said that he was gay?" This pastor's response was, "Love makes the world go round. All we need is love." His response was frustrating to me, because he was incorrect in that he was simply trying to provide a politically correct, inoffensive response.

However, something beautiful has occurred to me. The Word tells us that you have been equipped for every good work prepared in advance for you to do. You have what you need to pass the test. It may feel as if you have taken a knife to a gun-fight, so to speak, but if you are a parent, and your child is dealing with this issue, you have a weapon for the battle: it is love. Not the sappy, silly, superficial sort of love, but the kind of powerful, overcoming, life-changing love described in His Word. This kind of love is never rude or self-seeking, and does not delight in evil but rejoices in truth. This love always has hopes, always perseveres. It never fails.

You keep loving that child, by His definition, with all your might. He is strong in your weakness and He has all the answers to this test...actually they are written on His hands.

Lord, You are always the answer. As I imagine a child writing the answers to a difficult exam on his palm, I see a tiny, fragile hand with human answers only partly there because our nerves have caused us to sweat away the most crucial parts. But then I imagine You— holding open Your mighty, strong hand, and the answers there will never fade. Love. I love You more than my words can convey.

PRAYER JOURNAL

The topic of homosexuality isn't merely a debate or a trending controversy; it is heartbreak, and there can be victory.

_____

_____

_____

_____

_____

_____

_____

_____

_____

Flee from sexual immorality. All other sins a person commits are outside the body, but whoever sins sexually, sins against their own body.

I Corinthians 6:18

Candy Gibbs

Be careful with the words you use when talking to your teen about homosexuality.

_____

_____

_____

_____

_____

_____

_____

_____

_____

_____

_____

_____

Gay teenagers have a very high rate of suicide. Pray for your teen, his or her friends, and acquaintances.

Finally, all of you, be like-minded, be sympathetic, love one another, be compassionate and humble.

I Peter 3:8

_____

_____

_____

_____

_____

_____

_____

_____

_____

_____

We must do the best we can to raise our children, and we must take responsibility for our own shortcomings.

Candy Gibbs

And the LORD said, "I will cause all my goodness to pass in front of you, and I will proclaim my name, the LORD, in your presence. I will have mercy on whom I will have mercy, and I will have compassion on whom I will have compassion."

Exodus 33:19

_____

_____

_____

_____

_____

_____

_____

_____

_____

_____

Surround yourself with supportive people.

Rescue Prayer Journal

The LORD is gracious and righteous; our God is full of compassion.

Psalm 116:5

_____

_____

_____

_____

_____

_____

_____

_____

_____

_____

_____

_____

The real issue is that we want our children to love the Lord.

Candy Gibbs

But you, Lord, are a compassionate and gracious God, slow to anger, abounding in love and faithfulness.

Psalm 86:15

_____

_____

_____

_____

_____

_____

_____

_____

_____

_____

_____

Pray for your friends who have homosexual children; they need your compassion and support.

Your compassion, LORD, is great;
preserve my life according to your laws.
Psalm 119:156

_____

_____

_____

_____

_____

_____

_____

_____

_____

_____

When Jesus landed and saw a large crowd,
he had compassion on them, because they
were like sheep without a shepherd.
Mark 8:2

7

Praying for Your Teen to Take a Pro-Life Stand

"The thief comes only to steal and kill and destroy; I have come that they may have life, and have it to the full."

John 10:10

"'For I know the plans I have for you,' declares the Lord, 'Plans to prosper you and not to harm you, plans to give you hope and a future.'"

Jeremiah 29:11

I've sat in many a room with young women, most of them teenagers, as they weigh their "options," and the life of their unborn baby literally swings in the balance. There is such darkness there, as the enemy unleashes his attack with a vengeance. "Who do you think you are? You cannot do this. You are disgusting. No one will ever want you— your boyfriend doesn't even want you now. Your parents will hate you. You are an embarrassment. You are a slut and a loser. These people know it; but more importantly, you know it."

But then something amazing happens: the Word of Life, the Giver of Life, the Breath of Life is there. He pushes back the lies and the darkness and creates beautiful space. Space enough for that scared young girl to breathe and to come to the end of herself. I think that might be His favorite place to stand: where the roads of Best Effort and Human Reason intersect and we find the end of ourselves. He's always there. I have watched Him remind young women and families time and time again that life begins and ends in

Him. Life is sacred and valuable, and The Lord always provides a way. I have seen hundreds of girls—through deep, heart-wrenching, heart-cleansing sobs—choose life for themselves and their child.

What I am praying for our teens is that they would find that place at the end of themselves before there is a baby to consider. There are the same moments for teens who are not facing an unplanned pregnancy—moments when the enemy's attack is just as dark and full of vengeance. Moments when he declares to our children, "You are stupid and you were a mistake. No one wants you. No one has ever wanted you. You are worthless and your life does not matter." And again, the Word of Life Himself, the Light of the World, pushes the darkness aside, sits next to our teens and whispers, "Life is my gift to you. I have come that you may have life to the full."

Lord, may our teens have an understanding that all life is precious. "We are your dream," as my dear pastor, Jimmy Evans, would say. Thank You that a few moments with You are all we need for clarity and understanding, and that in Your presence is fullness of joy. Thank You, Father, for Life. May we live ours in such a way as to bring You great glory. We love You.

PRAYER JOURNAL

Let us say "yes" to life and not death. Let us say "yes" to freedom and not enslavement to the many idols of our time. In a word, let us say "yes" to the God who is love, life and freedom, and who never disappoints.

Pope Francis

_____

_____

_____

_____

_____

_____

_____

Abortion can feel like the
unpardonable sin. It is not.

Rescue Prayer Journal

Before I formed you in the womb I knew you, and before you were born I consecrated you....

Jeremiah 1:5a

_____

_____

_____

_____

_____

_____

_____

_____

_____

_____

Isolation is a tactic of the enemy to keep us in darkness so that we weaken.

Candy Gibbs

For we are his workmanship, created in Christ Jesus for good works, which God prepared beforehand, that we should walk in them.

Ephesians 2:10

_____

_____

_____

_____

_____

_____

_____

_____

_____

_____

The Word tells us that life is
. valuable and precious, and that the Lord
ordains life.

I praise you, for I am fearfully and won-derfully made. Wonderful are your works; my soul knows it very well.

Psalm 139:14

_____

_____

_____

_____

_____

_____

_____

_____

_____

_____

But when He had set me apart before I was born...and had called me through His grace.

Galatians 1:15

Candy Gibbs

Lo, children are an heritage of the Lord:
and the fruit of the womb is His reward.
Psalm 127:3

_____

_____

_____

_____

_____

_____

_____

_____

_____

_____

_____

Abortion isn't unforgiveable; it's just
irreversible.

In him we have redemption through his blood, the forgiveness of our trespasses, according to the riches of his grace....
Ephesians 1:7

_____

_____

_____

_____

_____

_____

_____

_____

_____

_____

Don't rush into decisions. The Lord has time. He isn't in a hurry and is never late—no matter what you need rescue from.

And are justified by his grace as a gift, through the redemption that is in Christ Jesus, whom God put forward as propitiation by his blood, to be received by faith. This was to show God's righteousness, because in his divine forbearance he had passed over former sins. It was to show his righteousness at the present time, so that he might be just and the justifier of the one who has faith in Jesus.

Romans 3:23-26

_____

_____

_____

_____

_____

_____

When your teen is facing a life-altering crisis, wait. Let the initial waves tame a bit, and then you will be able to hear the Lord better.

8

Praying for Communications with Your Teen

"To answer before listening—that is folly and shame."

Proverbs 18:13

Communicating with our children is one of the most important things we do each day. It is not "fact gathering"—but rather, it is truly connecting and understanding what makes them tick, what excites them, what upsets them, and what brings them hope. Communicating is choosing to focus in on their facial expressions. It's studying the crease he gets between his eyebrows when he's stressed, or the twinkle she gets in her eyes when she talks about her kitten.

Communication is fighting the urge to solve her teenage friendship problems, but instead allowing her to talk herself through to her own solution. It is teaching him to drive and being thankful for the laughter and screams you share together as he learns. It's believing he could play in the major leagues even on the days he can't get out of the batter's box. It is believing she will someday make a house a home as you pick her socks up off the bathroom floor for the 100th time.

Remember, relationships are a two-way street, and your children (yes, even your teens) want to know and under-stand you. Although it may take a while for them to admit it, you are their hero and they want to feel connected to you and valuable to you. Communicating is far more than fact-finding. It is throwing a rope from your heart to theirs and then pulling it in close.

As parents, we have some of the most precious, just-between-us experiences with our children. I love that when Madi is playing volleyball, I can see her look my direction out of the corner of her eye and I know just what she is thinking. I love that I end almost every text to Jake with "4," and only he and I know the significance of that. Those things are so dear to me because I can almost read an article in your mind about their day by simple watching how they walk to the car after school. You can know that when difficult topics present themselves—and they will—you will be able to communicate with your teen.

Lord, help us to truly know and connect with our children. We don't want to be deceived about who they are or what struggles they face. Also Father, You know I like to swim in the deep waters, not just splash around near the shore. It takes communication to move from the shallow and meaningless to the deep and powerful, and with it comes our ability to touch the hearts of our teens. Help us not to settle with wading. We want to swim. We love You.

I hope you will give it a shot. Here's a question for you to get you started:

What is your favorite time of the day, and why?

PRAYER JOURNAL

Teenagers can be prickly. They are often uncomfortable with communication because they are still learning how to do it.

_____

_____

_____

_____

_____

_____

_____

_____

_____

Let us then approach God's throne of grace with confidence, so that we may receive mercy and find grace to help us in our time of need.

Hebrews 4:15-16

Candy Gibbs

Our kids desire not only to talk to us, but for us to talk to them. Open communication necessary for a healthy family, but it is our children's wish as well.

_____

_____

_____

_____

_____

_____

_____

_____

_____

_____

_____

"The LORD would speak to Moses face to face, as one speaks to a friend."
Exodus 33:11

Communication is priceless, but certainly
not always pretty.

_____

_____

_____

_____

_____

_____

_____

_____

_____

_____

*My dear brothers and sisters, take note of
this: Everyone should be quick to listen,
slow to speak and slow to become angry.*
James 1:19

Candy Gibbs

Communication in any circumstance—having the nerve to stand face-to-face with another and take time out of our busy lives to address what is going on in the relationship says, "I love you enough. You matter to me."

_____

_____

_____

_____

_____

_____

_____

_____

_____

From the fruit of their mouth a person's stomach is filled; with the harvest of their lips they are satisfied. The tongue has the power of life and death, and those who love it will eat its fruit.

Proverbs 18:20-21

Rescue Prayer Journal

Children spell love T-I-M-E.

_____

_____

_____

_____

_____

_____

_____

_____

_____

_____

_____

_____

*We have spoken freely to you...and opened
wide our hearts to you.*
2 Corinthians 6:11

Candy Gibbs

Make time to know your teen and stay
connected to them. Time moves so
quickly, and you'll not want to look back
and wish you had done things differently.

_____

_____

_____

_____

_____

_____

_____

_____

_____

*May these words of my mouth and this
meditation of my heart be pleasing in your
sight, LORD, my Rock and my Redeemer.*
Psalm 19:14

Rescue Prayer Journal

Honesty with your teen is important because we want them to be comfortably opening up about their own struggles.

_____

_____

_____

_____

_____

_____

_____

_____

_____

_____

_____

Be open with your teen and share your own struggles when the opportunity presents itself.

9

Praying for and Mentoring Your Teen

"When they had crossed, Elijah said to Elisha, 'Tell me what I can do for you before I am taken from you?' 'Let me inherit a double portion of your spirit,' Elisha replied.

'You have asked a difficult thing,' Elijah said, 'yet if you see me when I am taken from you, it will be yours—otherwise not.'"

2 Kings 2:9-10

"Then I will give you shepherds after my own heart, who will lead you with knowledge and understanding."

Jeremiah 3:15

I pray frequently for adults who have any level of influence over my teenagers. Teenagers need adults other than their parents to look up to, to talk with, and to confide in. It is so important for us as parents to pray that the Lord will bring the right adults, and then to pray for those adults as they minister to our teens.

Your family may not be like mine, but have you ever had the experience of having shared wisdom and deep conversation with your teen over something they were struggling with and been met with rolling eyes and a shrug—only to have your teen burst through the front door just days later and proclaim that their youth pastor had solved everything and said exactly the same wise words you had shared days before that fell on deaf ears?! Sometimes our teens need to hear the same advice we've given them coming from other adults as well. Somehow it seems to go down more easily when they hear it from others.

In all seriousness, I encourage you to pray diligently about any person who may act as a mentor to your teen in any capacity. That person will carry influence with your teen, and you must be sure that each mentor shares your values and understands what you as parents are saying regarding specific issues. You do not want your teen to play the two of you against one another. Also, it is important to be clear that the relationship between your teen and any mentor is not a "friendship." The two are not peers and the mentor must understand that he or she is adult and is being looked to by the teen for guidance.

In the lives of my own teens, coaches have played a huge role as mentors. Madi has a sweet young woman who coaches her in volleyball who was also our babysitter all of Madi's younger years, so the two are very close. I love that Madi has a beautiful Christian woman to look up to and learn from.

Jake is an athlete who loves many sports. He has been greatly blessed with several coaches who challenge him, not only physically, but emotionally and spiritually.

We are all playing a role in training our teens in the way they should go. I love teenagers. They are truly the joy of my soul. I believe it is paramount importance to insure that they have godly adults around them to help keep them on track and moving forward.

Lord, we thank You for mentor relationships. Thank You for those just a little further down the road from us who can encourage us to keep moving as well as warn us about potholes along the way. This journey of life that You created and the fellowship with other believers was a beautiful plan. But You knew that all

Candy Gibbs

PRAYER JOURNAL

For even the Son of Man did not come to be served, but to serve, and to give his life as a ransom for many.

Mark 10:45

_____

_____

_____

_____

_____

_____

_____

_____

There is such value in having someone who is a little further down the road than you are, to give you the benefit of wisdom.

When Naomi heard in Moab that the LORD had come to the aid of his people by providing food for them, she and her daughters-in-law prepared to return home from there.

Ruth 1:6

_____

_____

_____

_____

_____

_____

_____

_____

_____

_____

Mentoring relationships are about passing the baton.

Therefore go and make disciples of all nations, baptizing them in the name of the Father and of the Son and of the Holy Spirit.

Matthew 28:19

_____

_____

_____

_____

_____

_____

_____

_____

_____

_____

It is important that the adults who hold sway with your teen share the same core principles as your family, what a valuable resource.

Likewise, teach the older women to be reverent in the way they live, not to be slanderers or addicted to much wine, but to teach what is good. Then they can urge the younger women to love their husbands and children....

Titus 2:3-4

_____

_____

_____

_____

_____

_____

_____

_____

The impact mentor relationships can leave on both the mentor and the mentee can last a lifetime, even if the relationship is only for a season.

Candy Gibbs

Know also that wisdom is like honey for you: If you find it, there is a future hope for you, and your hope will not be cut off.
Proverbs 24:14

_____

_____

_____

_____

_____

_____

_____

_____

_____

_____

_____

Help your teen think through people in their life whom they respect and who might be a good mentor for them.

And Jonathan made a covenant with David because he loved him as himself.4 Jonathan took off the robe he was wearing and gave it to David, along with his tunic, and even his sword, his bow and his belt.

I Samuel 18:1

_____

_____

_____

_____

_____

_____

_____

_____

_____

Allow your teen to be mentored, encourage them to talk with other people.

Jonathan said to David, 'Go in peace, for we have sworn friendship with each other in the name of the LORD, saying, 'The LORD is witness between you and me, and between your descendants and my descendants forever.' Then David left, and Jonathan went back to the town.'

1 Samuel 20:42

_____

_____

_____

_____

_____

_____

_____

_____

Trust that another person may be able to meet your teen in places that are hard, and support these relationships.

10

Praying for Your Teen and Pornography

"I have made a covenant with my eyes, never to look lustfully at a girl."
Job 31:1

"For as he thinketh in his heart, so is he...."
Proverbs 23:7 (KJV)

"Be self-controlled and alert. Your enemy the devil prowls around like a roaring lion looking for someone to devour. Resist him, standing firm in the faith....And the God of all grace, who called you to his eternal glory in Christ after you have suffered a little while, will himself restore you and make you strong firm and steadfast."
1 Peter 5:8-9a, 10

"No temptation has seized you except what is common to man. And God is faithful; he will not let you be tempted beyond what you can bear. But when you are tempted, he will also provide a way out so that you can stand up under it."

1 Corinthians 10:13

My co-workers and I were just discussing this: Be self controlled and alert, because your enemy prowls around like a roaring lion looking for someone to devour. There was a time when the enemy had to be much more cunning to and sneaky, to disguise himself. He could influence us, but it was more challenging for him. However, our culture has so plummeted that now he can brazenly walk right through the front door in all his filth, and evil, and we barely bat an eye.

Pornography has been a trap of the enemy for generations. In the American culture, just a few short years ago, there was certainly porn addiction, but it required a lot more effort for someone to fall into it. One would have to visit a porn store on the edge of town, walk up to the counter, and purchase the porn in clear view of others. Today, pornography is readily available even to children, free of charge and in complete privacy. There are no safeguards—that is, unless parents take their parenting seriously and stand against it.

Step one for parents is to realize that it is as easy for them to be lured into pornography as their teens. I believe that pornography is one of the most prevalent and powerful temptations facing Christian men today. Women are succumbing to the temptation as well with the outrageous infatuation with books and movies like 50 Shades of Grey. It is porn. You simply can't excuse it and it isn't up for debate. The stand starts with us; we are certainly the ones raising (or lowering) the standards in our own homes.

We must draw a line in the sand for our children: no pornography—not in our home, not at our school, not in our church, not in our community, not in our country.

Not on our watch.

Lord, we take captive every thought of our sons and daughters and we bind their will to the will of Christ. We thank You Lord Jesus that they are more than conquerors and will not be tripped up or overcome by the common or uncommon attacks of the enemy. They are about their Father's business and do not have time or energy for distractions. They are children of purpose and with a pure heart and the call of God on the souls they will advance and take ground for the Kingdom. No more messing around with the wiles of the enemy. These are men and women of valor with a warriors heart—a hearts that beat fast after their righteous King. We love You.

Candy Gibbs

PRAYER JOURNAL

For though we live in the world, we do not wage war as the world does. The weapons we fight with are not the weapons of this world. On the contrary, they have the divine power to demolish strongholds.

2 Corinthians 10:3-5

_____

_____

_____

_____

_____

_____

_____

Pray for your teen—they are inundated with sexual images, crude language, and a multitude of hostile attacks on our faith.

We demolish arguments and every pre-tension that sets itself up against the knowledge of God, and we take captive every thought to make it obedient to Christ.

1 Corinthians 10:6

_____

_____

_____

_____

_____

_____

_____

_____

_____

We must wise up. Our children must never be allowed to use their technology devices in private.

No temptation has overtaken you that is not common to man. God is faithful, and he will not let you be tempted beyond your ability, but with the temptation he will also provide the way of escape, that you may be able to endure it.

1 Corinthians 10:6

_____

_____

_____

_____

_____

_____

_____

_____

_____

Be open and talk to your teen about the damage pornography causes.

I made a covenant with my eyes not to look lustfully at a young woman.

Job 31:1

_____

_____

_____

_____

_____

_____

_____

_____

_____

_____

_____

Scripture memory and a close relationship with the Lord are the best weapons your teen has against pornography.

Candy Gibbs

But I say, walk by the Spirit, and you will not gratify the desires of the flesh.
Galatians 5:16

_____

_____

_____

_____

_____

_____

_____

_____

_____

_____

_____

There is simply no substitute for spending time as a family—make memories together; time passes so quickly.

For all that is in the world—the desires of the flesh and the desires of the eyes and pride of life—is not from the Father but is from the world.

1 John 2:16

_____

_____

_____

_____

_____

_____

_____

_____

_____

_____

Pray about finding a filtering system that is a good fit for your family.

As obedient children, do not be conformed to the passions of your former ignorance.
1 Peter 1:14

_____

_____

_____

_____

_____

_____

_____

_____

_____

_____

Put to death therefore what is earthly in you: sexual immorality, impurity, passion, evil desire, and covetousness, which is idolatry.

Colossians 3:5

11

Praying for Your Teen and Their Future

Almost every morning, the Lord reminds me to pray for parents. You can rest assured that I also pray over my husband, Brian, and myself as we raise our family. One of my prayers is that we would raise children of influence. For so many years in our nation, we (the body of Christ) have retreated and been afraid that our children would fall to peer pressure. Fear is never a good motivator. The spirit of fear never comes from the Father. Actually, the Word tells us that He has not given us a spirit of fear, but power, love and a sound mind (2 Timothy 1:7). How many of us would shout hallelujah to that "sound mind" as we deal with media, technology, and peer pressure in the lives of our teens? We are raising our children to follow the ways of the Lord, yet we doubt and worry that maybe He will forget us—forget them.

We have so many questions. How do I insure that my teens don't fall to peer pressure? How can I prevent my children from being negatively impacted by this culture? What if all of a sudden my family becomes aware of what I already know—that I don't know what I'm doing?!

Simply, we teach our teens to be the influence—to be the ones who are influencing their peers.

A few years ago Brian and I took our two youngest children, Jake and Madison, to see Princeton University. One afternoon our family visited a historic establishment where many Princeton alumni have studied. It's customary for people to carve their names into the tables, and as we were looking around we saw the names of many influential people spanning decades—Einstein, Bill Frist, and many more. That same day we took a wonderful tour of the campus of Princeton, which ironically began as a Christian seminary. I was blown away by the history and nostalgia. It has become one of my favorite family memories: how Jake and Madi took it all in. As we sat down for a meal, I imagined how incredible it would be if one of our children attended Princeton, and then immediately I had the thought, "But I would never want one of my children to attend here."

Most professors today are extremely liberal, and in general universities do not support Christian values. It was overwhelming to imagine that Princeton, a university founded on Christian principles, does not currently even hold a biblical worldview. Later that night, Brian and I sat in the tap room and it was a solemn moment. My thoughts were, "Why wouldn't I want my children to attend Princeton? Why couldn't our approach be: We are going to put you in unique situations, expose you to information, train you spiritually, strengthen and equip you so that you might go to Princeton or wherever the Lord leads you and be an influence of change. Be a world changer."

Our approach as parents changed that night from, "How do we keep them from being influenced?" to "How do we train them to be the influence?" It is time for us as parents to stop being motivated by fear and to understand the power that we have through the Word of God to equip our children to be who God has called them to be.

May I tell you that, as a mother, I know how emotionally overwhelming it can be to raise teens? I will concede that many nights I have kissed my kids good-night and then cried myself to sleep over something that will have they have to overcome. But we are not those who will be governed or motivated by our emotions; we will choose to be governed and moved by the very Word of God.

That being said, we must understand the fact that our children will be different in the world, and that they may sometimes feel left out. We certainly do want our children to be "different." They have been sanctified, to make an impact—to leave a mark on this earth. I want your teens to leave some footprints behind letting the world know they took some ground for their King!

Lord, I thank You that You hem our children in and that You have laid Your hand on them (Psalm 139:5). You have unique and exciting plans for each of them. I ask You, Lord, to increase our faith as parents to love, support, and encourage them to take boldly the ground You have set before them. Whatever Your plans are, we know they are good. Lord, help us train our teens to flex their spiritual muscles, stretch themselves in their faith, and stand for what they believe in. We trust You completely for their destiny. We love You.

PRAYER JOURNAL

Your beginnings will seem humble, so
prosperous will your future be.

Job 8:7

_____

_____

_____

_____

_____

_____

_____

_____

_____

_____

Our job is simply to strengthen them spiritually, teach them to love Him first and .
love others as themselves.

"For I know the plans I have for you," declares the LORD, *"plans to prosper you and not to harm you, plans to give you hope and a future."*

Jeremiah 29:11

_____

_____

_____

_____

_____

_____

_____

_____

A goal is a dream that has been pondered. Time has been taken to think it through and our teenagers have considered the steps it will take to fulfill. Then they must get to it! Hard work and persistence do pay off!

No, in all these things we are more than conquerors through him who loved us. For I am convinced that neither death nor life, neither angels nor demons, neither the present nor the future, nor any powers, neither height nor depth, nor anything else in all creation, will be able to separate us from the love of God that is in Christ Jesus our Lord.

Romans 8:37-39

_____

_____

_____

_____

_____

_____

_____

Just because the plan isn't your plan,
doesn't make it the wrong plan.

Candy Gibbs

Pray continually.
Thessalonians 5:15

_____

_____

_____

_____

_____

_____

_____

_____

Setting goals and focusing on the horizon is also a way that we gain enjoyment of this life we live. If our teen's focus is on the dust under their feet as they pound out their course each day, they will become discouraged and exhausted. But if our young people take time to lift up their heads and focus on their goals in the distance, they will certainly notice the beauty of their surroundings and the pleasure of their traveling partners, as well.

Posterity will serve him; future genera-
tions will be told about the Lord.
                                    Psalm 22:30

_____

_____

_____

_____

_____

_____

_____

_____

_____

_____

_____

Our children are only ours for a short time,
and even then we hold them with an
open hand.

Candy Gibbs

Know also that wisdom is like honey for you: If you find it, there is a future hope for you, and your hope will not be cut off.
Proverbs 24:14

_____

_____

_____

_____

_____

_____

_____

_____

_____

_____

_____

The purposes and callings of our children
are not our responsibility.

Consider the blameless, observe the upright; a future awaits those who seek peace.

Psalm 37:37

_____

_____

_____

_____

_____

_____

_____

_____

_____

_____

Only the Lord knows what He had designed for our children to accomplish and it is outside of my control.

12

Building an Ark

"My whole life I have been complaining that my work was constantly interrupted until I discovered that the interruptions were my work. "

Henry Nouwen

One of my dearest friends shared this quote with me recently, and it really spoke to me! Life is busy and full. Life is exciting and overwhelming. Life brings great joy and deep sorrow. Life is often beautiful and safe, and yet it can be ugly and frightening. Life with teenagers can be all of those things before lunch time!

Each morning I have a list of things to do before day's end, as I'm sure many of you do. As busy couples with on-the-go involved families running from one event to the next, it can be enough to make our heads spin. I have often joked that my schedule can be so tight on some days that getting 5 minutes behind in the morning stretches to running an hour behind by 5:00. And then there are all those interruptions.

I have spent some time asking the Lord about it, and His response to me was, "You get your calendar so full that if I want to thrill you, bless you, or get your attention, I simply must interrupt." Ouch.

Some of the most beautiful interruptions of my life have been—

1) A 5-year-old boy calling to be picked up sick from school. I was supposed to be in an interview, but instead Tanner and I spent the afternoon watching cartoons and coloring. Though he's a man now, a husband

and a daddy himself, and I still re-member it like it was yesterday.

2) A call at 11:00p.m. that something was wrong with my mom. I was supposed to be leaving on a cruise the next morning but instead my family and I walked my momma Home.

3) A 6:30a.m. wakeup call and a 9:00a.m. doctor's appointment on the days that Jake and Madi were born. I was supposed to be work-ing, but instead I was introduced to two of the most important people in my life.

4) An unexpected visit from my son on a Saturday night announcing that I would soon become a grandmother. I was supposed to be just hanging out with my nieces, but the Lord gave me a gift of peace and hope for new beginnings.

Interruptions are the joy of life.
Interruptions break up the mundane
routine of life and remind us that He is not
bound by our to-do list or our calendar.
The Lord has a standing appointment
and can enter the scene unannounced.
And aren't we so thankful!

Think of Noah. He was a righteous
man living life with his family while
the world went crazy all around him—
and then the Lord interrupted. Noah, I
want you to build an ark for your family
and I want you to do it exactly the way
I describe it to you. The Ark will be a
shelter for you and your sons when
unfamiliar disaster strikes. There will
be a day that it will flood, but when the
waters rise and firm ground for your
feet to stand on is a distant memory, the
Ark will hold what you hold most dear
and I will be your protection.

"Noah did everything just as God

commanded him."

Genesis 6:22

So amidst the busy and the uncertain, remember to build the Ark for your family. Because when the flood comes and the waters rise, the Ark will be a shelter for you and your family. When the waters rise and firm ground for your feet to stand on is a distant memory, the Ark will hold what you hold most dear and He will be your protection.

Lord, You are our refuge and strong tower. You are the Ark to which we run and are saved. We trust our families to You, Lord, and we are thankful for the plans and purposes You have for them. May You be glorified in our homes, Father. We will see You on the waves. We love You.

PRAYER JOURNAL

Thank God for His presence—it is a life preserver in the truest sense, holding us up
even when the waves come crashing in
on us.

_____

_____

_____

_____

_____

_____

_____

_____

_____

_____

For I know the plans I have for you,
declares the Lord.

Jeremiah 29:11

Candy Gibbs

Ask God to begin revealing His callings
and purposes for your family.

_____

_____

_____

_____

_____

_____

_____

_____

_____

_____

_____

*Fathers...bring them up in the training
and instruction of the Lord.*
Ephesians 6:4

Rescue Prayer Journal

God isn't hiding from us, but He does love
to thrill us and to be found.

_____

_____

_____

_____

_____

_____

_____

_____

_____

_____

_____

The calling of your teen is unique to him
or her.

Many nations will come and say, 'Come, let us go up to the mountain of the Lord, to the temple of the God of Jacob. He will teach us his ways, so that we may walk in his paths.' The law will go out from Zion, the word of the Lord from Jerusalem.

Micah 4:2

_____

_____

_____

_____

_____

_____

_____

_____

_____

_____

Pray that your teen will be a leader and influence the culture around them.

*Whenever I bring clouds over the earth
and the rainbow appears in the clouds, I
will remember my covenant between me
and you and all living creatures of every
kind. Never again will the waters become
a flood to destroy all life.*

Genesis 9:12-15

_____

_____

_____

_____

_____

_____

_____

_____

_____

Pray that your teen will fear God and seek
righteousness.

Candy Gibbs

God will never abandon us or allow us to become lost in a sea of troubles.

_____

_____

_____

_____

_____

_____

_____

_____

_____

_____

Trust in him at all times, you people;
pour out your hearts to him, for God is
our refuge.

Psalm 62:8

Rescue Prayer Journal

The Lord commands to oceans—He walks
on the water, and even the winds and
waves obey Him!

_____

_____

_____

_____

_____

_____

_____

_____

_____

_____

Build your ark, piece by piece, truth upon
truth, standard upon standard, to protect
your family.